ASIAN HOLIDAYS

by Faith Winchester

Bridgestone Books

an Imprint of Capstone Press

Fast Facts

- Asia is the world's largest continent.
- Asia has every kind of climate from tropical to polar and from desert to rainy.
- China has more people than any other country.
- Japan is made up of four main islands and many more small islands.

Bridgestone Books are published by Capstone Press • 818 North Willow Street, Mankato, Minnesota 56001
Copyright © 1996 by Capstone Press • All rights reserved • Printed in the United States of America

Library of Congress Cataloging-in-Publication Data
Winchester, Faith
    Asian Holidays/by Faith Winchester
    p. cm.--(Read-and-discover ethnic holidays)
    Includes bibliographical references and index.
    Summary: Briefly describes eight festivals celebrated by Chinese, Japanese, and Vietnamese, including various New Year's festivals, Ch'ing Ming, and Buddha's birthday.
    ISBN 1-56065-458-9
    1.Holidays--Asia--Juvenile literature. 2. Asia--Social life and customs--Juvenile literature.
    [1. Holidays--Asia. 2. Asia--Social life and customs.] I. Title. II. Series.
GT4872.A2W55 1996
394.2'695--dc20
                            96-25909
                               CIP
                               AC

Photo credits
Lynn Seldon, cover. Index Stock, 8. FPG, 12, 18. Beryl Goldberg, 20.
Unicorn/Florent Flipper, 4; Robert Baum, 6; Ron Jaffe, 10; Aneal
    Vorha, 14; Betts Anderson, 16.

Table of Contents

Words in **boldface** type in the text are defined in the Words to Know section in the back of this book.

Asians

The term Asian refers to people who have come from the continent of Asia. This includes such countries as China, Japan, Vietnam, Laos, Cambodia, and many others. China once ruled much of the area.

In addition to the solar calendar, some Asian countries follow a lunar calendar. This means their months are based on the cycles of the moon. A lunar month is 29 and 1/2 days long.

Many Asians follow Buddhism. It is a religion and way of life. It was started by a man called Buddha. Buddhists **meditate** to become perfect. Some Buddhists give up everything to devote their lives to their religion. They are called monks.

Red is a lucky color for Asians. It means happiness. Asians like to celebrate. They have many holidays. The Chinese invented fireworks. Now fireworks are an important part of celebrations around the world.

Many Asians live in their own ethnic communities. This community is in Toronto, Ontario, Canada.

Chinese New Year

The Chinese New Year is celebrated between January 21 and February 20. It is an important holiday. The Chinese prepare for a whole month. This preparation is called Little New Year. They clean the house and make food. They hang a picture of Tsao-Chin. He is the god of the kitchen. One week before New Year, they burn his picture. This sends him to the spirit world to tell about the family's hard work.

On New Year, families celebrate with feasts and fireworks. They wear new clothes and hang a new picture of Tsao-Chin. The celebration lasts for five days. Many relatives visit. Children receive red envelopes filled with money. There is a Dragon Dance in the street. A dragon costume is made from paper and cloth. Many people can stand inside the costume. The dragon twists and turns.

The Lantern Festival starts 10 days later. It lasts three days. Money is collected for a charity.

The Dragon Dance and fireworks are part of this Chinese New Year festival held in Philadelphia, Pennsylvania.

Ch'ing Ming

Ch'ing Ming means the pure and bright festival. It is celebrated exactly 106 days after the winter solstice. This is the day in December when the days start to get longer instead of shorter. Ch'ing Ming celebrates the beginning of spring.

Three days before Ch'ing Ming, the Chinese people turn off their stoves. They will eat only cold food until the holiday.

Ch'ing Ming is the Chinese memorial day. Everyone visits the graves of **ancestors**. It is a time for respect. They clean the area around the graves. They bring food and small gifts to offer to the dead. After they pay their respects, they eat a big picnic feast. Sometimes this is called the Feast of the Dead.

Some Chinese families plant a new tree on this holiday. It is a way to remember the dead and celebrate spring.

Ch'ing Ming is a time to remember ancestors.

Japanese New Year

The New Year is an important time for the Japanese. They begin to prepare the last week of December. They wrap presents and plan family reunions. They make food that will taste good and look pretty. They try to pay off all of their bills.

Houses are decorated with evergreen and bamboo. The evergreen represents stability in times of change. The bamboo represents honesty.

The celebration starts on New Year's Eve and continues until the middle of January. It is a time for families to get together to visit and play games. Some Japanese businesses close. Families exchange gifts. They eat **traditional** dinners together.

Many families visit a temple on New Year's Eve. On that night, a **gong** is rung 108 times. Buddha taught that people have 108 weaknesses. Ringing the gong represents clearing away the weaknesses. The people can start the new year without them.

The Japanese New Year is a time of celebration and family.

Buddha's Birthday

Buddha was born around 563 B.C. in India. He was a prince and had a lot of money. Buddha wanted to take away all human suffering. He left his home and money to meditate. He taught people to live good lives. His followers started the religion of Buddhism after he died about 463 B.C.

Buddha's birthday is celebrated on April 8. It has been observed by Buddhists everywhere for more than 1,300 years. Buddhists visit shrines and wear special robes. They **chant** and honor Buddha.

The night before Buddha's birthday is the time to clean the statues and shrines. The statue of Buddha is blindfolded so he cannot see the cleaning. This happens only once a year.

Sometimes this holiday is called Hana Matsuri in Japan. This means Festival of the Flowers. Buddhists take flowers to the shrines and offer them to Buddha.

Some Asians give flowers to Buddha for his birthday.

Tet

Tet is the Vietnamese New Year. The word means "the first day" in Vietnamese. This is the most important holiday of their year. The festival lasts for seven days.

Only good things must happen during the festival. What happens then will determine how the rest of the year will be. Broken things must be fixed. People who are mad at each other should forgive each other. The attitude of visitors can determine if the year will be happy and prosperous or not.

Tet is a time for relaxing and having fun. It is important to spend time with family. It is a time to be proud of your culture. It is like a memorial day to remember Vietnam.

Tet is also a time to remember ancestors. The Vietnamese believe the spirits of their ancestors are present during Tet. They are honored at a family altar. When Tet is over, the spirits go back to the spirit world.

Only good things must happen during the Vietnamese Tet.

Doll Festival

The Doll Festival is for Japanese girls. It takes place on March 3. It is also called Hina Matsuri.

Girls display their doll collections. The dolls are very special and expensive. They put their dolls on boxes or boards set up like a staircase. The stairs are covered with a red cloth. On the top of the stairs are two special dolls. They represent the Emperor and the Empress of Japan. These dolls wear royal clothes.

Any doll furniture a girl may have is set up with her dolls. Sometimes the displays are decorated with peach blossoms. The doll displays are often set up many days ahead of time.

Girls dress up in their best holiday clothes. They go visiting to see other doll displays. The girls get together for tea parties in front of the displays. They drink tea and eat little cakes.

Girls keep their dolls even when they marry. They will be passed on to their own little girls.

Very expensive, special dolls are displayed during the Doll Festival.

Boys' Festival

Boys' Festival is held on May 5 in Japan. It is similar to the Doll Festival for girls. Parents use this holiday to teach their children good values. They want their children to be brave and strong.

Boys set up doll displays for Boys' Festival, too. But their dolls are warriors. They are dressed in war clothes and have weapons. Instead of having tea parties, boys have traditional wrestling matches.

Outside their houses, parents of boys set up tall flagpoles. They hang large cloth or paper fish from them. The number of fish is the same as the number of boys in the family. The fish are decorated in bright colors. The fish are carp. Carp are brave enough to jump over waterfalls.

In recent years, Boys' Festival has also been called Children's Day. The name was changed to make the holiday include girls as well. But no matter what it is called, the holiday is still for boys.

Boys' Festival in Japan honors the boys in a family.

Harvest Moon Festival

Many Chinese people do not live by a lunar calendar anymore. But the moon is still very important to Chinese life. The Harvest Moon Festival is celebrated in the fall. It is celebrated when the moon is full. People thank the moon for the good harvest. They ask the moon for a good harvest again next year.

The Harvest Moon Festival lasts only one day. The Chinese eat moon cakes as part of the celebration. Moon cakes are round like the moon. They are sweet.

There is no traditional ceremony for the Harvest Moon Festival. Families usually take the day off from work. They eat a large dinner together. Moon cakes are part of the meal.

Sometimes families have a ceremony to capture the moon. They catch the moon's reflection in a bowl of water.

A Harvest Moon Festival in New York celebrates the harvest.

Hands On: Make a Red Envelope

During the Chinese New Year, children receive red envelopes filled with money. They get them from their parents and relatives. You can make and decorate red envelopes for your money.

You will need
- red construction paper
- tape
- a sticker
- ruler
- scissors

1. Use the ruler to measure a square. All the sides should be the same length. Make your square from five to eight inches (13 to 20 centimeters) long on each side.
2. Cut the paper along your measurements.
3. Fold the paper in half from corner to corner. Open it back up again. Fold the paper in half again from the other corners. The fold will look like an X.
4. Take one corner and fold it to the middle.
5. Fold the next corner to the middle. Tape along the edges that meet.
6. Turn the paper and fold the next corner to the middle. Tape along the edges that meet.
7. The flap that is left is the top. When you have filled your envelope, fold the top down and seal it with a sticker.

Pronunciation Guide

Buddha	boo-dah
Buddhism	bood- is-um
Hana Matsuri	hah-nah maht-su-ree
Hina Matsuri	hee-nah maht-su-ree
Tet	teht
Tsao-Chin	tah-ho chin

Words to Know

ancestor—relative who came before
chant—singsong way of speaking
gong—metal disk that makes a sound when hit
meditate—think very hard
traditional—handed down from generation to generation

Read More

Buell, Hal. *Festivals of Japan*. New York: Dodd, Mead, 1965.
Cohen, Hennig and Tristam Potter Coffin. *America Celebrates*. Chicago: Visible Ink Press, 1991.
Hou-tien, Cheng. *The Chinese New Year*. New York: Holt, Rhinehart and Winston, 1976.
McGuire, William. *Southeast Asians*. New York: Franklin Watts, 1991.

Useful Addresses and Internet Sites

Asia Resource Center
110 Maryland Avenue NE, Suite 70
Washington, DC 20002

Asia Society
725 Park Avenue
New York, NY 10021

Celebrate Chinese New Year
http://www.dae.com/cny/
Children's Day
http://www.wakhok.ac.jp/~nobuaki/japan.html

Index